STARTING YOUR BUSINESS THE POSITIVE WAY

Starting your business the positive way

A guide to successfully starting and running a small business

ANNA BARWICK

Anna Barwick

CONTENTS

CONCLUSION

DISCLAIMER

| 1 |

FOREWORD

What a brilliantly rounded starter book for anyone thinking of setting out on their own in business. If you have already ventured forth, it can only assist you on your journey to success with some helpful self analysis tips too.

I particularly love how Anna gives an overview of everything to consider in business, explaining all the aspects simply and clearly with some really important do's and don'ts.

I've witnessed many people's businesses fail due to cash flow problems and no forward business planning, or even an understanding of where their business is 'at' on a regular basis. This book will empower you to do your best to avoid these potential pitfalls.

Anna also includes the importance of a positive and success mindset. I cannot recommend working on this enough and being mindful of any thoughts and beliefs that may block your path to success. I personally know two former dragons from the tv series Dragons' Den and they have both said to me independently that one of the reasons entrepreneurs fail is due to their negative and self limiting beliefs.

Everyone deserves to be happy and successful in all aspects of their lives and if you're a budding or existing entrepreneur then *Starting Your Business The Positive Way* is a must-read.

Sue Stone
Author, speaker and transformational leader
TV Secret Millionaire

| 2 |

INTRODUCTION

When I originally qualified as a Chartered Certified Accountant I was always attracted to working in industry and the opportunity to be involved with a company, rather than just their financial aspects.

After becoming involved with an industrial company as finance director and co-owner, I spent over 25 years actively involved in all aspects of growing this company and seeing it flourish into a multimillion pound business before selling it to a large group.

I decided to put my experience to good use by setting up a small accountancy practice dedicated to helping small businesses and start-ups become more efficient and successful. It was at this point that I realised how little practical and straightforward advice there is for those considering, and taking the first steps to, setting up their own business.

This guide is intended to help those of you that are wondering if working for yourself is the right move by looking at the main aspects to consider before taking the plunge.

It is not intended to provide complete details of all the legal and other requirements but is rather an overview to guide you towards the areas you need to research in more detail. The information in the book relates to the laws of England and Wales, but the general principles can easily be adapted for any country.

| 3 |

WHY START YOUR OWN BUSINESS?

What makes you want to start your own business?

It may seem an odd question to be asking but let me be honest from the start and tell you that starting out on your own will not be easy and there will be many times when you will be wondering why you left the security of paid employment.

That is why I always ask the budding entrepreneur to start their journey by asking themselves this question and make sure they establish in their mind what it is that makes them really want to do this and really want to succeed.

The actual reason itself could be any number of things:

- A strong desire to be your own boss
- Realising there is an untapped market for a product or service
- A lifetime ambition

- Wanting to make a difference

These are just a few of many reasons why people set out on their journey of going it alone, and when times get tough, as they invariably will, it is important to keep these reasons in mind and remember why you are doing this.

An obvious reason for working for yourself is the desire to reap the benefits and profits of your hard work and effort. This is a very valid reason and one that should probably be on everybody's list. Once you are working for yourself you are taking all the risks and should therefore be prepared to accept all the rewards.

The other question I ask is what type of person you are. Are you willing to take a risk? Are you willing to take full responsibility for the outcome? Are you willing to work all hours and put your other commitments aside for the success of your business? Do you have a positive mindset and total belief in yourself and your business? Again, these are necessary traits when things get tough.

I would also ask yourself, why is now a good time to start the business? It could be that you have spotted a market opportunity and with the right research this is a very good reason indeed. You may be facing redundancy and have decided to "go it alone". This may be a good opportunity to pursue your dream but bear in mind what I mentioned above and make sure you are the right person to run your own business and that this is not just an alternative to job hunting, because if it is you are unlikely to succeed.

Finally, you will most likely need to invest a certain amount of money in the venture. Are you prepared to, and can you afford to, lose this money should the business fail. Or if you have to borrow to get started, how will you repay the loan if the business fails? You may by now be thinking that everywhere else in this book I talk about having a positive mindset and that you should have a total belief in yourself and your ability to succeed; however, while that is true, you have to first ensure that what you are embarking on is viable and also that you are able to deal with the consequences should the worst happen.

By now, if you are still reading, you have probably decided that running your own business is right for you, and the following chapters will go through the practicalities of what you need to do next.

| 4 |

SELF-EMPLOYED OR COMPANY?

When you start your business the most usual structures will be to work as self-employed (sole trader) or as a company. There are other alternatives, such as partnerships and limited liability partnerships but they are more specialised, and I will be concentrating on the first two in this book.

To briefly explain, working as a self-employed person requires no formal set-up and you can just start working and earning money. If things do not work out for you, then you can just stop trading and go back to employment (you will of course need to declare any income you earned in the self-employed business to HMRC and pay the relevant tax). A partnership is basically two or more self-employed people working together with an agreement in place as to how to share the profits etc. Alternatively, you may choose to set up a private limited company. This requires a formal set-up and has legal requirements attached to it, including the need to officially close it down should you decide things are not working out. It also has several benefits such as potential tax savings and removing risk from you as an individual.

If you are not sure which route to take, it is quite possible to start off self-employed and then incorporate the business (create a limited company) further down the line when the business grows.

Self-employed

This is the easiest way to start your business. You simply start trading and whatever is left after you have covered your bills is yours to keep.

There is no formal need to set up your business, although if you decide to use a business name (rather than just trading in your own name) you should check to make sure it has not been registered as a trade name and that there is not another local business of the same name.

You are not an employee of the business, although you can employ staff. Any profit the business makes will be yours and you should declare it on your annual self-assessment. All the assets owned by the business are legally yours, and all liabilities and debts are also legally yours.

If you are not already registered for self-assessment with HMRC then you should do so no later than 5th October following the first tax year in which you are trading. A tax year for self-employment runs from 6th April until the following 5th April, although you can choose a different year end for your business if you prefer. Once registered, you will receive a Unique Taxpayer Reference (UTR) which you need for submitting your self-assessment.

Limited company

A limited company is the other usual way to start trading. When you form (incorporate) a limited company, you create what is known as a separate legal entity. What that means, in basic terms, is that the company exists separately from you as an individual and it owns its own assets, unlike when you trade as self-employed when you own everything yourself.

Aside from potential tax savings, it has the advantage of protecting you from any personal liability should the business fail, and should you decide to sell the business later, this can relatively easily be achieved by the sale of your shares.

The potential disadvantages include the fact that all assets and profits belong to the company, and you need to decide on the most tax efficient way of extracting the cash. Where you are a sole shareholder and director this is relatively simple, but something to bear in mind, nevertheless.

In order to set up a limited company, you need to incorporate it with Companies House. No two companies can have the same name, so you need to search to ensure the name is not already taken before you start.

All companies also need to have a Memorandum and Articles of Association. The Memorandum of Association is a document that details the initial shareholders of the company and their agreement to form the company, and the Articles of Association is a document detailing the rules agreed by the shareholders and directors as to how the company should be run and the relative powers of each. The Articles can be what is known as "model" Articles, which is a standard set of rules that most companies that have no special rules adopt when incorporating. These can be added to or replaced by other Articles, but either way it is important for you to be aware of their content to make sure you comply with them.

Once the application is accepted by Companies House, you are given a Company Registration Number, which you must display on all official documents. You will also receive an Authentication Code which you need to keep accessing your account online for the purpose of filing an annual Confirmation Statement and for any changes you may need to make in future.

Unlike individuals, who pay income tax and national insurance, companies pay corporation tax, which tends to be lower and one of the main reasons for people going down the route of forming a company. Once you have incorporated your company with Companies House, you will receive a Unique Taxpayer Reference (UTR) for the company, and you will then need to register for corporation tax with HMRC.

Directors and Shareholders

A limited company needs to have at least one director and one shareholder. Another company can be either or both, although you do need to have at least one person as a director. You also used to need to appoint a company secretary, i.e. a person responsible for ensuring the company complies with the law and carries out its administrative duties, but that is no longer necessary.

Directors and shareholders are often confused with each other, especially in small companies where it is common for one person to be both. There are, however, distinct differences between the two roles:

Shareholders

Shareholders are the owners of the business. They have no say in the day to day running of the company although they have got the right to call a meeting to vote on matters where they disagree with aspects of how the directors run the company.

Shareholders can be directors as well, although they do not have to, and they receive a return on their investment in the company by way of a dividend.

Directors

Directors are the people appointed to run and manage the company through the Board of Directors. They have authority to make decisions on the company's behalf and can be either executive or non-executive directors. Executive directors are internal employees of the company who are engaged in the day to day running of the business, whereas a non-executive director is an external person, brought in to provide an independent view to the Board. There is no requirement for private companies to have non-executive directors and most small companies have just one or more executive directors.

Directors do not need to be shareholders and as such are not entitled to dividends unless they also hold shares. It is most usual for directors to be paid through payroll as employees.

As I mentioned above, it is very common for small companies just starting out to be owned and run by the same person, and therefore the boundaries between the two roles are necessarily blurred. It is nevertheless important to understand the distinction, as there may well come a point as the company grows where you will want to take on additional directors and/or additional shareholders may come along to invest in your company.

Shares

The most common type of shares in a small company is an ordinary share. These rank equally for voting and for dividends. It is possible to set up a company with a single share, although I always recommend at least 10 shares, and preferably 100, even if there is only one shareholder setting up the company as this makes it easier at a later date should another investor come along. Where there is only one share in place, this then needs to either be split or additional shares need to be issued.

It is possible to set up different classes of ordinary shares that rank for dividends independently (often known as "ABC shares"), but this needs to be done carefully so as to ensure it complies with company law.

There are other types of shares, such as preference shares, that can be issued by a company. These are shares that rank for dividends before the ordinary shares, usually at a fixed percentage rate of the profit of the company.

Dividends

Dividends are the return on investment received by shareholders in proportion to their shareholding (or according to the specified rules in the Articles). They can only be declared and paid out of distributable profit and reserves, which means that there has to be sufficient profit in the company in order to be able to legally pay a dividend.

For a small business owned and managed by one or two people the big advantage of being a limited company is the favourable tax rate on dividends.

| 5 |

FUNDING THE BUSINESS

One of the first things to do when you have decided that running your own business is for you is to decide how much money you need to get started. You need to make sure you have access to enough cash to get you started and to keep going until you start earning money and beyond. You also need a good idea of how much your regular outgoings will be and what your chances are of covering these and making a profit.

Cash Flow

Cash is king! This old adage is never truer than when you run your own business. Many profitable businesses have gone under due to a lack of cash, and therefore the inability to pay their bills when due. This may seem strange, because surely if you are profitable you have enough cash? Unfortunately, this is not always the case: many businesses have their funds tied up in things such as stock and debtors, and their ability to pay is tied into what is called the cash flow (or working capital) cycle.

The cash flow cycle is an explanation of how funds go through the various stages in the business before being turned back into cash. The first stage is the investment of money into stock and the time the stock is held before being sold. The second stage is the amount of time customers take to pay for the goods they have bought from you. This amount of time is reduced by the amount of time your suppliers allow you to pay for the goods bought.

This cycle is very important to bear in mind, especially if your intended business is going to be supplying goods of any kind, or indeed if you need to invest in products to provide a service, as you will need to ensure you have access to enough funds to cover this cycle without running out of cash.

To do the calculation, you will need to make a best estimate of the number of days it will take you to sell any stock you buy. If you are going to offer credit to your customers, you then need to add the number of days you will give the customers to pay. Finally, if you can set up credit terms with the suppliers of stock, you take away the number of days credit they give you.

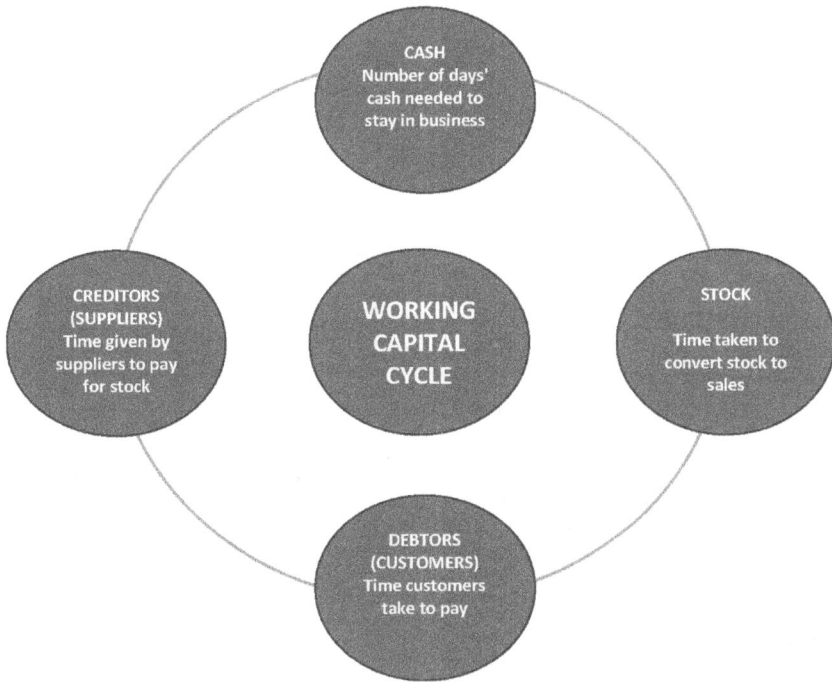

The number of days you end up with indicates how long you will need to invest the money you are putting into stock before it is converted back to cash. For a business that relies on selling products this is a crucial measure, whereas for a service business it is of course of less relevance.

When starting up you will also typically need to invest in a certain number of items needed to run your business. These items, known in accounting terms as fixed assets, are those that enable you to do your work but do not in themselves convert directly into cash. They are therefore a long-term investment, and include things such as machinery, vans/cars, computer equipment, office furniture etc. Whilst they are a one-off purchase, it is nevertheless important to budget for everything you will need in advance. There will also be other costs that you may need to cover from the start, such as liability insurance, rent, professional subscriptions and data protection licences.

Finally, you will need to live in the short term until the business starts providing you with an income. Again, you should work out how much you need to live on and how long you realistically expect it to take before the business will be turning over enough to cover the costs.

Ideally, you should also have at least 3 months' savings over and above this to cover any unexpected downturns, but for a start-up business that is often unrealistic for a while.

Once you have calculated these amounts, you need to decide whether you have, or have access to, the necessary funds.

Funding

Maybe you will have sufficient savings to cover this. The benefit of this is that you do not need to involve anyone else, and if you are able to (and prepared to) survive without the funds, you are ideally placed to start your business on your own terms.

If you do not have enough funds personally, you may have family or friends that are willing to invest in your start-up. Once others are involved, it is important to make sure you have an agreement in place regarding the investment. When it comes to friends and family it is easy to be very informal, but often further down the line all sorts of disagreements occur, both where the business is not successful and where it is extremely successful. The kind of things you should agree in advance include what happens should the business fail, and the money be lost, the return (interest or profit share) the person advancing the money expects, if any, and also a time frame for when they expect to receive their money back.

If neither of the above sources are available, you will need to look to banks or other external investors for funds. This is a lot trickier these days as banks especially have ever tighter criteria for investing in new businesses. If this is the route you are going to go, then a good Business Plan will be imperative. It is highly unlikely that a bank or investment specialist will look at your idea without this. For more information about Business Plans see the separate Chapter.

| 6 |

OTHER CONSIDERATIONS

This aim of this short chapter is simply to touch briefly on a few other topics, some of which apply to all businesses, and others that will only apply to specific industries.

Insurance

Having good business insurance is necessary regardless of what you do. In these times of litigation, it is simply too risky to operate without it, and the cost for businesses in low-risk sectors can be very low. A lot of businesses are not allowed to operate without insurance cover. For those of you that deal with larger companies, you will probably find that adequate liability cover is a requirement for them to want to deal with you.

If you are an employer, you are required by law to have employer's liability insurance. This can usually be incorporated into your overall business insurance.

Health and Safety

Whatever type of business you operate, Health and Safety (H&S) will be relevant to you, both through legislation such as the Health and Safety at Work Act 1974 and through common sense.

Should you ever be unfortunate enough to be at the receiving end of a negligence claim, being able to show good H&S procedures, such as risk assessments, will go a long way towards a successful defence. And regardless of this, it will, of course, also help you, your staff and customers stay safe on a day-to-day basis.

I recommend you familiarise yourself with the above Act and also with your day-to-day H&S responsibilities. A lot of helpful material is available on the internet and through trade organisations.

IR35

IR35 will be relevant to you if you intend to work through a Personal Service Company (PSC) whereby you provide your services as a sole employee of a limited company.

The legislation aims to prevent persons that would have been employees of the client company had they not operated through their own limited company, from gaining tax advantages by doing so.

The gov.uk website considers a person not to be an employee if:

- *they're in business for themselves, are responsible for the success or failure of their business and can make a loss or a profit*
- *they can decide what work they do and when, where or how to do it*
- *they can hire someone else to do the work*

- *they're responsible for fixing any unsatisfactory work in their own time*
- *their employer agrees a fixed price for their work - it doesn't depend on how long the job takes to finish*
- *they use their own money to buy business assets, cover running costs, and provide tools and equipment for their work*
- *they can work for more than one client*

If you don't feel you can answer yes to most or all of this, then you should look into whether you may be impacted by IR35.

CIS

The Construction Industry Scheme (CIS) has been operating for several years now and applies to most trades that work as contractors or subcontractors in the construction industry. It was set up to avoid subcontractors doing work for cash in the construction industry with little or no records being kept and then "disappearing" before their self-assessment and tax was due. Instead, contractors are now obliged to keep records of their payments to subcontractors and deduct tax from their invoices before paying them. These amounts are then paid across to HMRC monthly, and the subcontractors can reclaim any overpaid tax at the end of the year through their self-assessment.

If you are a builder or tradesman who uses subcontractors or work as a subcontractor yourself, you should register with HMRC under CIS.

| 7 |

TAXES

Tax is an immensely complicated and involved subject, but in this chapter I will attempt to scratch the surface by outlining the main taxes that apply to a typical business based in England.

Income Tax

This is a tax paid by individuals. If you have decided to run your business as self-employed you will pay income tax on your profit by completing an annual self-assessment tax return and paying the tax in a lump sum by 31st January each year. If your tax is above £1,000 you will also be required to make payments on account on 31st January and 31st July each year.

Unlike limited companies, small businesses can choose to use cash basis for working out their income and expenditure.

Everyone gets a personal allowance, which is an amount that you can earn before you start paying income tax. This amount changes each financial year (6th April to 5th April) and the current basic allowance can be found online at gov.uk. The allowance is sometimes increased or decreased, depending on a number of factors, such as being able to claim for items such as clothing, or earning above £100,000 (at the time of writing this) when the allowance is reduced by £1 for every £2 earned above the threshold.

Income tax is paid at different rates: basic, higher, and additional. These rates are paid according to bands based on your earnings and, like the personal allowance, these bands change each financial year and can be found online at gov.uk. A common misconception is that once you reach a higher band you are taxed at the higher rate on everything. This is not the case. You pay income tax at the basic rate on income up to the higher rate, and then you pay tax at the higher rate on income above this.

For example, using the 2020-21 rates:

Band	Taxable income	Tax rate
Personal Allowance	Up to £12,500	0%
Basic rate	£12,501 to £50,000	20%
Higher rate	£50,001 to £150,000	40%
Additional rate	over £150,000	45%

Here, you would not pay income tax on your earnings up to £12,500 and would pay 20% on the next £37,500. If your total earnings were £87,500, you would then pay 40% on the final £37,500.

If your earnings exceed £100,000 it becomes a little more complicated as the personal allowance is reduced as mentioned above.

Income tax is also paid by employees. In this case the tax is collected, along with national insurance, each month under PAYE. If you have decided to set up a limited company and pay yourself through payroll this is the way you would be taxed on your personal income. The amounts payable under PAYE are the same as above, except that you are issued with a tax code which reflects your personal allowance. The number on the tax code is your personal allowance with the last digit removed, so if your personal allowance is £12,500 your tax code would be 1250L. The letters are used to indicate several things and are beyond the scope of this book, but you can again look online at gov.uk for a full explanation of tax codes.

If you chose to operate as a limited company, chances are that you, in addition to your monthly pay, will decide to take at least some of the profits of the company by way of a dividend. Dividends are also subject to income tax but are (at the time of writing) more tax efficient as they are taxed at a much lower rate than self-employed profits or salaries. Additionally, there is currently a dividend allowance, similar to the personal allowance, whereby the first £2,000 (in 2020-21) is tax-free.

If you are operating as a limited company and your only income is from a salary through payroll you are unlikely to need to also complete an annual self-assessment tax return, but if you have other income, such as from dividends, you are likely to need to do this. You would then deduct the tax paid through PAYE from the total amount of tax due.

Corporation Tax

Corporation tax is the tax paid by limited companies on profits. You could, in simple terms, say that it is the company equivalent of income tax for individuals.

Whereas self-assessments are always completed to 5th April each year, with the tax payable on 31st January (and payments on account on 31st July), companies set a financial year end of their own choosing and corporation tax is payable 9 months and 1 day after their year end.

Also, unlike income tax which is charged in bands according to income, corporation tax is currently (since 2014) charged at a single rate which, like income tax, is announced each year in the Budget. In the tax year 2020-21 the rate is 19% on net profit.

National Insurance

National insurance contributions are a tax paid by employees and employers, and the self-employed, in order to qualify for certain benefits and for state pension.

There are different types of national insurance, known as classes:

National Insurance class	Who pays
Class 1	Employees earning more than £183 a week (2020-21 tax year) and under state pension age – they are automatically deducted by the employer
Class 1A or 1B	Employers pay these directly on their employee's expenses or benefits

Class 2	Self-employed people earning more than £6,475 a year (2020-21 tax year) until they reach state pension age.
Class 3	Voluntary contributions - you can pay them to fill or avoid gaps in your National Insurance record
Class 4	Self-employed people earning profits of £9,501 or more a year (2020-21 tax year) until 6th April after you reach state pension age

As you can see, the class you pay is dependent on your employment status and how much you earn. Unlike income and corporation tax, national insurance is not an annual tax. This means that it applies in any pay period where your pay exceeds the Lower Earnings Limit. If you earn less than this limit in a subsequent month, you don't pay national insurance. By contrast, income and corporation tax are annual taxes. They work on a cumulative basis and consider the earnings/profits for the entire year, regardless of whether they were earned in regular amounts.

Company directors' national insurance contributions, unlike other employees, are usually calculated on an annual basis, as they can otherwise manipulate their monthly income in such a way as to reduce their national insurance contributions.

VAT

VAT is a tax on goods and services charged by VAT registered individuals, who can usually reclaim the VAT they have paid out for business purposes.

There are different VAT rates, the main ones being standard rated (currently 20%), zero-rated (0%) and exempt. If you become VAT registered, you should familiarise yourself with these rates, as it is important to apply the correct rates for your VAT returns.

Once your business reaches a certain threshold (2021: £85,000 over 12 months), it is mandatory to register for and charge VAT at the applicable rate. However, it is also possible to register voluntarily for VAT even if your turnover is below the threshold. There are several reasons why a business might want to do this. For example, suppose you will supply mainly VAT registered companies. In that case, they will be able to reclaim the VAT you will charge them on your sales, and being VAT registered yourself means that you will also be able to reclaim VAT on your purchases and expenses, thus saving you up to 20% (at the current rate).

For businesses up to a certain size there are also different types of VAT schemes, such as Flat Rate, which you may find is advantageous if you have very few outgoings with VAT. Typically this is applicable to someone working in a service industry with a home-based office. You should also consider whether to account for VAT on an accruals or cash basis. The former uses the figures from when you raise and receive invoices, whereas the latter is based on when you pay and get paid. As you can see, if you offer and receive credit terms, this can vary widely, but if you are paid on invoice and pay suppliers when ordering, then there is no difference at all.

Other Taxes

There are several other taxes, such as capital gains tax for individuals, and CIS deductions, all of which are beyond the scope of this book.

| 8 |

BUSINESS PLANNING

Setting out a Business Plan, however simple, is, in my opinion, one of the most critical parts of ensuring the success of your new business. If it is just yourself that is involved in the business, it does not need to be a formal document, but you should still sit down and run through the main areas of business planning. You should ensure you are thoroughly familiar with your market, your competition and the risks and advantages you are faced with as you grow your business. Suppose you are looking for any investment in your business. In that case, a Business Plan is essential, as it is unlikely that an investor, especially a bank, will take your business seriously without one.

Business planning is an area where there can be an advantage in involving an experienced business mentor, who will offer an independent view as to how achievable and realistic your plans and goals are. They will also help ensure that the figures used in the forecast are as accurate as possible.

In this chapter, I have set out a framework for a typical Business Plan. It is not a comprehensive manual for creating your Plan, and there are many excellent books specifically on this subject if you feel you want to learn more.

There is no right or wrong in what you include or how detailed you make your Plan, but you should consider who you are preparing it for and who will see it when you decide what goes into it.

The Business Plan

A typical Business Plan will contain any or all of the following subjects:

- *EXECUTIVE SUMMARY*
- *THE BUSINESS*
- *TARGET MARKET*
- *COMPETITION*
- *STRATEGY*
- *RESOURCES*
- *FINANCIALS AND FORECASTS*
- *RISKS AND OPPORTUNITIES*
- *CONCLUSION*

When you decide what information to include in the Plan, you should consider who the audience is and bear the following in mind.

A potential backer is concerned with:

- *Market demand risk*
- *Competition risk*

- *Strategic risk*
- *Financial risk*
- *Competitors*

Banks are mainly interested in what can go wrong and what you will do to mitigate the damage if things go wrong. As far as banks are concerned, you should be seen to be conservative, cautious and risk averse and forecasts should be readily achievable.

Key numbers that will be useful to potential backers:

- *Sales*
- *Growth*
- *Sales by segment*
- *Margin*
- *Net profit*
- *Market size*
- *Market share*
- *Market demand drivers*
- *Market demand growth*

Planning:

Before you start putting your Plan together, it is important to gather relevant data about your business segment. You will need various data *to* put together information that will be useful to you and others.

Data on market demand, size, drivers and growth trends will help you determine the sales and growth you are likely to achieve.

Data on competitors:

- *Size*
- *Location*
- *Turnover*
- *Profitability*
- *Positioning*
- *Competitive advantage*
- *Strategy*
- *Plans for the future*

This will give you valuable insight into how well you are placed against your competitors.

Customer Surveys:

These will tell you what customers expect from your business and your competition, which will help you understand what you need to provide to potential customers to succeed and stay ahead of the competition.

Once you have gathered this information, you are ready to put your Plan together.

The Business Plan in detail

Executive Summary

This is a short introduction to the business. It enables the reader to become familiar with the content of the Plan and the business without having to read the full document.

The Business

Introduction

At the start of this section is the introduction to your business. It should contain a few paragraphs that contain:

- *The name and location of the business*
- *The products and services you provide*
- *How you provide the products and services (e.g., shop, online)*
- *Main customer groups and geographical areas served*

Vision

The vision statement is a paragraph that explains where the business wants to be.

A lot of small businesses leave this out as it is not seen as necessary at their level. I can't entirely agree with this. I feel it is of utmost importance that anyone starting out on their own should have a vision and know what it is rather than just bumbling along, not knowing whether you are going in the right direction.

I suggest starting by sitting down and looking at where you see yourself in three, or even five years, from now. Setting this out on paper enables you to be aware of precisely what you are aiming for. It sets the focus, which can then be broken down into increasingly smaller parts and timescales. It allows you to identify the strategies, goals, and objectives that will enable you to achieve your vision.

Only when you know this will you be able to put into words your vision statement.

Mission and Values

These are optional statements to include in your Business Plan, depending on whether you feel including them adds to your business's understanding and whether your potential readers of the Plan will expect to see them.

A mission statement is a paragraph that describes why the business exists.

A value statement explains who the business is and what are its priorities and beliefs.

Basic financials

This introduction to the financials should contain a summary of either recent results or if you are starting out and have no trading history yet, an overview of how you intend to finance the business and how much you have already spent on setting it up.

Target Market

This is the most essential part of your Plan, regardless of whether you are doing this exercise for yourself or as part of a formal Plan to raise investment. Without thoroughly considering these questions, it will be challenging to know if your strategy is achievable and almost impossible to set realistic goals.

Market Size

For a small start-up business, this may be difficult to establish. Still, by looking at the volume and size of your competitors and your potential customers, in terms of numbers and turnover, it should be possible to identify your market size with some accuracy.

Market Share

Again, for a start-up, this is by necessity an estimate, but when you have done your homework of analysing the market and your strategy, you should have a reasonable idea of where you will be positioned and how big a share you will be able to obtain.

Market Demand

This may be quite difficult for a start-up business to accurately estimate, especially if you will be supplying a new product. However, if you are already working in your chosen industry, you should find this easier.

When estimating market demand, you should also consider whether your market is growing, contracting or stable, as this will have a profound impact on your forecast.

Risks and opportunities

Next, you should list the risks and opportunities your business is likely to face and the likelihood of them happening.

The risks to consider are those that could affect the viability of your new business. This could be in the form of market volatility, susceptibility to the general economy and any number of risks specific to your market sector. Conversely, it is equally important to consider the opportunities your business has and the likelihood of capitalising on them. This is probably an easier task, as you may well be starting your business venture due to having discovered one or more market opportunities. It is, however, worth spending time analysing whether there are other, less obvious, opportunities that could be successfully exploited.

Carrying out a Strengths, Weaknesses, Opportunities and Threats (SWOT) analysis is useful for doing the above exercise. This is done by identifying the top half dozen or so strengths, weaknesses, opportunities, and threats facing your business. You then look at what can be done to exploit the strengths and opportunities and minimise weaknesses and threats.

Strengths:

- *What advantages do you have over your competitors?*
- *What are your unique selling points?*
- *What resources do you possess that your competitors don't?*

Opportunities:

- *Are there new trends in your business sector that you can take advantage of?*
- *Are there changes in your market that will benefit you? E.g., changes in law or lifestyles of your customer base.*

Weaknesses:

- *Which areas could you improve on?*
- *Where do you lack resources compared to your competitors?*

Threats:

- *What can your competitors do to harm you?*

> • *What are the major threats in your market sector?*

A less well known but similar tool is Strengths, Opportunities, Aspirations, and Results (SOAR) Analysis, which focuses on the positives in your business and uses them to inform a strategy for the future.

The Strengths and Opportunities are as above.

Aspirations:

> • *What do you care deeply about?*
> • *What difference do you hope to make to your key stakeholders?*

Results:

> • *How will you know you are succeeding?*
> • *Identify 3-5 measures of success*
> • *What will be different what you have achieved your vision?!*

Competition

Respect the competition! This is a piece of advice I always give new entrepreneurs. It is too easy to focus solely on your own plans, but instead of dismissing or ignoring them, you should look at your main competitors and consider what makes them successful. Can you learn from their success? Compare their strengths with what you can offer. You should also consider how you are going to coexist with them in the market.

Equally importantly, you should consider your competitors' weaknesses and how you can exploit these weaknesses and profit from them.

To find this out, you should research the competition thoroughly and find out about their:

- *Sales*
- *Growth*
- *Profit margins*
- *Ownership*
- *Market segments*
- *Location*

It is easier said than done, especially for the smaller business, where the competitors may also be small enough not to be obliged to publish financial information. However, try to get as much information as possible to enable you to glean some insight into what makes them successful or otherwise.

New Entrants

When you have researched the competition and documented them in your business plan, you should look at the threat of new entrants into your market sector and area.

Are there others trying to break into your market, or is it relatively static? Again, you should consider this and how you will be more successful at grabbing more market opportunities than these new competitors.

Ease of Substitution

Where is your product or service pitched? And is it something that can easily be substituted? You need to consider whether what you supply is a commodity or whether the brand/supplier matter? This can work for or against you, depending on whether you are trying to break into a market by cost advantage or by quality and reputation. If your product or service is a commodity, you need to compete on price, whereas if the brand or your name is what people are paying for, the price will be less important, though probably still a factor.

Direct/Indirect Competition

As well as the direct competitors, you should also look at the indirect competitors. These are those that are not in the same line of business as you but who supply a product or service that can be either substituted for yours or is the same but supplied differently. For instance, you may provide products through an e-commerce site, but an indirect competitor might supply the same goods through stores where customers can see and touch the products. It is essential that you consider how you can compete against this. Maybe you can compete on price due to lower overheads or offer 30-day return terms.

So, to summarise, you need to consider the big risks and how you will mitigate them, your big opportunities that balance the risks, and how to exploit them.

Strategy
Strategy

This is a description of what your business does to meet its goals and objectives and the direction it takes to achieve them. You can look at the strategy as the medium-term road map for the business.

Having identified the vision for your business above, you should look at how you will achieve it by outlining a strategy to enable you to succeed.

For instance, if your vision is to run a £100,000 turnover photography business three years from now, the strategy will look at how you will achieve this. Will you work in a studio, on location, or both? Will you sell your work through galleries, online or at exhibitors, or will you do commission-only work? Your strategy should set this out, and also how you plan to improve your competitive advantage.

Goals and Objectives

A goal is a statement in words of what your business is aiming for.

An objective is a target in figures that helps measure whether the goals are being achieved. You may be familiar with the acronym SMART - a method for setting objectives, which stands for Specific, Measurable, Attainable, Relevant and Time-limited.

Your goals break down your strategy into specific sections, and the objectives set measurable targets and timescales for the goals.

Continuing our previous photography example, you may set a goal of opening a studio and another of setting up a website for selling your art. The objectives will quantify these goals and provide a timescale that you can then work towards.

By breaking the vision down into these increasingly smaller sections, you will be able to plan what you need to achieve and will be able to measure your actual achievements at any time against the overall Plan.

Resources

Demonstrate how your company will deploy its scarce resource to implement its strategy.

There can be many scarce resources in a business. The obvious is cash, but the workforce and product can also be scarce resources.

For instance, if you have the only key skills required to carry out your business's work, then its income and expansion depend entirely on your available hours. Consider how you will overcome this limiting factor. Can you buy in the skills by employing others with similar abilities, and if so, what would the impact your profit margin be? Can you bring the skill set through the business by training existing staff, and if so, how long will it take, and how much of your time will it take?

Another scarce resource that you may need to consider is product and/or components. Is there any likelihood of a product shortage, and if so, can it be sourced from alternative suppliers?

There are many other scarce resources, and these are just a couple of examples. You need to consider the scarce resources relevant to your business, and how you can overcome shortages.

Additionally, you should consider if your business has an abundance of scarce resources. You may have a competitive advantage because of possessing something your competitor(s) don't.

Once you have done this, you can document the big resource risks and opportunities that may impact on the achievability of your business plan.

Financials and Forecasts

The contents in this section are very much dependent on whether you are a new business about to start up, or if you are already trading.

If you have been trading for a year or more, you will be able to include your previous years' profit and loss accounts and balance sheets. This should be sufficiently detailed to provide meaningful information for your business, but not so complex as to make it difficult to trawl through. An example would be utility bills, which for most businesses could be presented as a single figure, unless, for instance, the business relies on a large water consumption which is peculiar to this industry and therefore needs to be shown as a separate item.

If you are just about to start your business, then you will, of course, not have historical data to show in this section, but it will be necessary to produce profit and loss, and cash flow forecasts whether you are a start-up or have been trading for a while.

The reason for this is that, while historical data is good, and certainly gives an idea of the size and profitability of the business it is, as it says, historical. A business plan is concerned with the future and so is any investor that will be reading it.

It is fine to show the previous year's results in the Plan, but if most of the turnover was achieved in the first quarter and has steadily contracted ever since, this will not be evident from the accounts and is therefore not valuable for a would-be investor. Nor is it useful to you as a decision-making tool.

It can be extremely daunting when faced with forecasting turnover, profit, and cash flow, but if you have done the research in the previous sections, you will be very well placed to start putting together a forecast.

How to prepare profit and cash flow forecasts are covered in more detail in Chapter 7, but for the purpose of the Business Plan, you should consider the period that is relevant to the Plan. If your strategy and content of the Business Plan is based on a 5-year period, then a 3-month forecast is clearly not going to be appropriate. Typically, forecasts will be based on 1 to 5 years, depending on the business and the purpose of the business plan.

Risks and Opportunities

The purpose of this final section is to set out the big financial and business risks and opportunities that may impact on the business plan.

Essential a summary of the SWOT (Strengths, weaknesses, opportunities, and threats), this section further explores the main risks and opportunities that are likely and unlikely to lie ahead for the business.

Having already identified the risks and opportunities that could have a major positive or negative impact on the business and its future, this is where you go into detail of what the likely outcome of something happening (or not happening) would be and quantify the impact if it does (or does not). You should also go a step further and explore what you can do to mitigate any risks or maximise any opportunities.

A classic example is a business that is planning to sell trendy umbrellas. A significant and obvious risk to this business would be if the country were then facing a long, hot summer and a drought. What effect would this have on the financial forecasts, how big is the risk, and what could be done to mitigate it? Maybe diversifying and selling trendy swim/beach wear as well might be one solution.

Conclusion

At the end of the Business Plan, you should summarise the highlights of what you have discussed in the previous sections to draw the reader's attention to the main points and reiterate them, so they are not overlooked among all the other information. Even if you are writing the Plan for yourself, this is an excellent way to end the exercise, as it will make you concentrate on finding the parts that will be most important to you.

| 9 |

EMPLOYING STAFF AND PAYING YOURSELF

Sole Trader

If you decide to start out as a sole trader, your income will be the money you make from the business. This means what is left after deducting all your expenses from your income.

You do not put yourself on a payroll, although you may decide to draw a set amount from the business bank account each month (your "wages") and leave the rest invested in the business. Whichever way you decide to pay yourself, you will be liable for income tax on the full amount of profit you make, regardless of how much you take out of the business.

This is one of the reasons why efficient tax planning is essential, and why many businesses are set up as limited companies, where tax can often be minimised more easily.

If you start employing staff, you will have to set up a payroll, operate a PAYE scheme, and pay them through this. Your own pay remains outside the payroll. To set up a scheme, you need to register with HMRC and run the payroll for your staff weekly, fortnightly, or monthly. You also need to submit an RTI for each period to HMRC. This is an electronic summary of the employees' pay and deduction, which tells HMRC the amount you need to pay across to them by the 22nd of each month. If you are a small employer (under a certain threshold), you can make payments quarterly instead.

There is a lot of commercial payroll software available on the market. Some of the cloud-based accounting software includes a basic payroll for businesses with only a few employees. HMRC also have free software that can be downloaded from their website for very small businesses.

Limited Company

The same principle applies as above regarding the payroll. The only difference is that in a limited company, you are now an employee just like any other staff and you will also be paid through payroll. The profit the company makes is after deducting your (and the other employees') salary and other expenses, and it is taxed on this net profit.

Employing Staff

In addition to the payroll aspect of employing staff, you incur several other obligations as an employer. This section discusses some of the main requirements but is not an exhaustive list, and you should check with websites such as gov.uk and ACAS for detailed information about your responsibilities before employing any staff.

For instance, all staff are entitled to a payslip, written terms of employment, a minimum wage, paid holiday, parental leave and pay and, of course, decent working conditions. As an employer, you are also required to register under auto-enrolment, provide a pension scheme and make contributions (currently 3%) towards your staff's pension (subject to certain exceptions).

You are also liable for Employer's National Insurance contributions above a certain limit. This is currently 13.8%, so it can add a substantial amount to the overall staff costs. Many small employers qualify for what is known as Employment Allowance, which means they do not have to pay Employer's National Insurance until the contributions reach a certain amount (currently £4,000).

| 10 |

BOOK-KEEPING, BUDGETING/ FORECASTING AND ACCOUNTING

For many start-up businesses, keeping adequate accounting records is low on their set of priorities. I urge you not to be one of those businesses and to keep on top of this right from the start.

Why Keep Books?

Book-keeping and accounts is such a large topic that easily fills a book in its own right, but it is fundamental to the success, and survival, of any business that you have an outline understanding of keeping books and interpreting them. That way, you will know if you are profitable, and it will assist you in making the right decisions in your business.

Far too many businesses, new and established alike, are too busy existing to make time to review their performance on an ongoing basis. They leave it to the end of the year to hand all their financial information to their accountant to provide a set of accounts, hoping that the year will have been profitable. While many companies survive like this year after year, it depends entirely on luck rather than strategic planning, and is extremely risky, particularly in harder times, such as recessions.

Aside from the risk factors of not keeping on top of the financial performance of your business, it also means that you are not measuring if you are working efficiently and at your most profitable. A typical example is a business that provides, say, three different services. One may be very profitable; one may break even, and the last one may be losing the business money. If you run your business without looking at the financials, you may continue for years making a modest profit simply because the profitable service is carrying the other two. With proper financial analysis, this would be identified, and you would be able to look at the two services that are not contributing and decide if they can be changed in a way that will make them profitable or if they should be scrapped. Either decision will make the company more profitable without any additional work or marketing required and is achieved simply by staying on top of your financial analysis.

Basic Ledgers

At its most fundamental, any business needs to keep records of its income and expenditure in order to meet their legal obligations and complete their tax returns.

This involves keeping a note of the money you earn from your business and keeping records of the expenses you incur, including invoices and receipts to back it up.

Basic ledgers are simply book-keeping methods of recording this income and expenditure for further analysis in the accounts. At its most basic, it is done by hand in a book (a ledger), although these days, it is typically done in a spreadsheet or by using computerised accounting software. It is worth noting that the UK is moving towards MTD (Making Tax Digital), where it will soon (by 2023) be a legal requirement to keep books by electronic methods.

Whichever method is used, the principle is the same, and this principle is the age-old double-entry book-keeping. The idea behind it is based on debits and credits and the principle that when all entries have been made in the ledgers, the debits and credits will balance.

It is beyond the scope of this book to teach double-entry book-keeping in its entirety and in any depth (this is the subject of one of my forthcoming books), but any business owner needs to have a fundamental understanding of recording transactions and of interpreting the results.

Income & Expenditure Account

The simplest and cheapest method of recording transactions when you first start out in business is to keep a simple income and expenditure account, either by hand or, more commonly these days, in a spreadsheet.

Your ledger, either way, consists of two sides: your income on one side and your expenditure on the other. If all your transactions go through a business bank account, this is very easy to do and quite simply requires you to list all the transactions from your bank statements into your ledger. At the end of each period (daily, weekly or monthly, depending on the volume of transactions), you can then balance your ledger to the balance on the bank account to ensure you have recorded all the transactions.

The example below shows a typical and simple way of recording your transactions into a spreadsheet. A manual ledger will work on the same principle.

Month	Details	Income	Products	Chair Rent	Mobile Phone	Saturday Girl	Equipment	Accountancy
January	Income	320.00						
	Income	360.00						
	Income	315.00						
	Chair Rent			100.00				
	Chair Rent			110.00				
	Chair Rent			150.00				
	Colours		70.00					
	Colours		100.00					
	Colours		50.00					
	Mobile				45.00			
February	Income	195.00						
	Income	307.00						
	Income	220.00						
	Income	200.00						
	Chair Rent			60.00				
	Chair Rent			90.00				
	Chair Rent			100.00				
	Chair Rent			50.00				
	Colours		10.00					
	Colours		20.00					
	Colours		40.00					
	Colours		30.00					
	Saturday Girl					20.00		
	Saturday Girl					20.00		
	Saturday Girl					20.00		
	Mobile				45.00			
March	Income	325.00						
	Income	198.00						
	Income	250.00						
	Income	393.00						
	Chair Rent			100.00				
	Chair Rent			90.00				
	Chair Rent			90.00				
	Chair Rent			110.00				
	Colours		100.00					
	Colours		30.00					
	Colours		60.00					
	Colours		117.00					
	Equipment						20.00	
	Mobile				45.00			
April	Income	90.00						
	Chair Rent			50.00				
	Accountancy fee							125.00
		3,173.00	627.00	1,100.00	135.00	60.00	20.00	125.00

If part of your business is cash-based, i.e., you either receive or make payments by cash, then recording this is a little more complicated and requires a few additional columns in your accounts, depending on whether you keep a petty cash float.

Petty Cash

The traditional, and still the best, way of using cash for buying minor items is through an imprest petty cash float.

Example:

You draw out, say, £100 and put it in a float (a cash box for instance). When you need to purchase something, you take the appropriate amount out of the cash box and replace it with a receipt for the goods. Therefore, at any one time:

Cash in box + receipts in box = £100 (the original amount)

When the money in the box runs low, or at the end of the month, you take out the receipts and replace them with an amount of cash equivalent to the total value of the receipts.

The details of the receipts are then entered into either a petty cash ledger or an additional column in the main income and expenditure ledger.

Cash Takings

If you receive part or all your income in cash, I strongly recommend banking the actual amounts of the takings rather than random amounts.

This way, you can link banking to the daily receipts, and the book-keeping becomes much less complicated.

Some businesses use part of their cash income to pay for expenses directly, and while that is certainly possible to account for, it is a lot more complicated and beyond the scope of this book.

Computerised Accounting Software

Th cost of accounting software has come down dramatically in recent years. With the expansion of the internet, user-friendly online software (e.g. Xero, FreeAgent and Quickbooks) aimed at non-finance professionals is now affordable for most smaller businesses.

Using software for your accounts not only overcomes the requirements for MTD (Making Tax Digital), but it also simplifies book-keeping and allows bank transactions to feed directly into the software, thereby saving a lot of manual input work.

Cash vs Accruals Accounting

When you first start out in business, if you are operating as a sole trader, you may well find that using what is known as cash accounting is the easiest way of calculating profit and completing your tax return.

As the name implies, you simply take the figures from your income and expenditure account, add up all the money received in the year, and subtract all the payments made in the year to arrive at your annual profit.

As your business grows above a certain level (currently a combined turnover of more than £150,000 p.a.), and/or you are operating as a limited company, you will instead need to use what is known as accruals accounting.

When you need to produce statutory accounts, these must follow several accounting principles and policies. One of these is the accruals principle. The accruals principle states that all income and expenditure should be accounted for in the period to which it relates.

For example, you will need to account for income in the year the sale took place rather than the year the payment was received. Similarly, the expenditure should be accounted for in the year that the expenditure was incurred rather than when you paid for it.

A typical example is if you pay for your business insurance annually midway through the year. In cash-based accounting, the whole amount will be offset against the profit for the year, whereas in accruals-based accounting, only the proportion relating to the financial year the accounts are being prepared for should be considered.

Example:

> Company year-end is 31st December. Insurance of £500 for the year starting 1st July paid 30th June. Six months, i.e. £250 (£500/ 12 x 6), should be accounted for in the year to 31st December, with the rest accounted for in the following year's accounts. This will be shown in the accounts as a prepayment towards the next year.

Similarly, if you pay your utility bill quarterly in arrears, and the next bill is not due until two months after the year-end, you should accrue for one month in the accounts.

Example:

> Company year-end 31st December. The electricity bill for the quarter to the following 28th February comes to £150.
>
> As this includes the month of December, but the invoice is dated in the following year, you need to make an accrual for one month, i.e., in this case, 1/3, so £150/3 x 1 = £50.
>
> This should be shown in the accounts to 31st December as an accrual.

Profit vs Cash

I stated earlier in the book that "cash is king" and that is very true for any business. However, we need to understand the difference between profit and cash and the importance of both when running a successful business.

Cash, in business terms, is the actual liquid funds a business has available in the bank or elsewhere at any one time. It was discussed earlier in the context of the working capital cycle.

In a straightforward business with little or no stock and no credit terms offered to customers, cash and profit will equate to almost the same thing. You make sales and get paid, and you pay for your expenses. What is left in the bank at the end of the month or the year is your cash reserve and profit.

The lines start to get blurred when you start offering credit to customers and receiving goods and services on credit. If you then also hold stocks of goods, you can soon end up in a situation where your cash and your profit are no longer in any way similar.

For instance, say you make one major sale for 100,000 and to fulfil the contract, you need to purchase goods for £40,000. You have made a healthy profit of £60,000 and, on the surface, are doing exceptionally well. However, say you had to offer the customer 60 days to pay for the invoice to win the contract, but your supplier insists on payment in 30 days. In this situation, you are extremely profitable, but unless you have access to £40,000 at the end of month 1 you are facing potential bankruptcy.

At the other extreme, you may have initially invested, say, £20,000 to start up your business. You then make lots of cash sales daily and purchase the goods on credit. If the sales price of an item is £10, but the materials you need come to £8 and you then have rent etc, to pay, you may find that each item makes a net loss of £1. Because you have cash in the bank, are receiving cash for each sale and have negotiated credit terms with your suppliers, you can probably keep the business going for quite a long time before eventually running out of cash, all the time blissfully unaware that you are making a loss because you keep seeing a positive bank balance.

As you can see, either scenario will end in disaster for your business, and steps should be taken to avoid either. The main areas to look at to stay profitable and have a positive cash flow are:

- *Get your pricing right. Don't just look at covering the cost of materials. Make sure your pricing will cover all your overheads and leave enough for you to live on with a surplus to expand the business and see it through any slow periods*

- *Make sure you match the terms you offer your customers to the terms offered to you by your suppliers. If you allow your customers 30 days to* pay, then negotiate at least 30-day terms with your suppliers so your income and outgoings coincide

- *Keep up to date cashflow forecasts, and, if possible, aim to have sufficient funds to keep the business going for 3 months*

- *Keep management accounts. In a small business that could be as simple as looking at the monthly profit and loss account with comparatives for the previous period that your accounting software produces*

Financial Accounts

When you are first starting out, all the different financial terms and reports can be rather overwhelming, but these are the main reports you are likely to come across:

Profit & Loss Account

This is one of the two main reports in financial accounting, and very important as it shows income and expenditure laid out in a format that provides information about turnover, gross profit and net profit.

It is usually produced monthly, quarterly, or annually, and often includes a column showing comparative periods from the same period in the last financial year.

Profit and Loss

For the year ended 31 March 2022

	2022	2021
Turnover		
Other Revenue	-	3,500.00
Sales	32,886.92	5,583.36
Total Turnover	32,886.92	9,083.36
Cost of Sales		
Purchases	1,950.00	-
Total Cost of Sales	1,950.00	-
Gross Profit	30,936.92	9,083.36
Administrative Costs		
Advertising & Marketing	8,711.46	-
Audit & Accountancy fees	140.88	-
Bank Fees	30.00	-
Cleaning	99.23	-
Consulting		3,600.00
Entertainment 100% business	44.86	
General Expenses	418.33	8,000.00
Light, Power, Heating	551.08	730.57
Motor Vehicle Expenses	649.29	-
Postage, Freight & Courier	94.19	-
Printing & Stationery	83.87	512.00
Rent	3,937.52	-
Repairs & Maintenance	886.30	-
Subscriptions	1,234.80	
Telephone & Internet	164.46	-
Travel - National	230.75	-
Total Administrative Costs	17,276.64	12,842.57
Operating Profit	13,660.28	(3,759.21)
Profit on Ordinary Activities Before Taxation	13,660.28	(3,759.21)
Profit after Taxation	13,660.28	(3,759.21)

Balance Sheet

This is the other of the two main financial statements. The balance sheet is a summary of all the assets your company owns, and all the liabilities. These are balanced by the owners' equity (capital).

The balance sheet is based on the Accounting Equation:

Assets – Liabilities = Capital

Assets can be fixed (long-term) or current (short-term). Fixed assets are capital items with a remaining life of more than one year. Typical examples are furniture, computer equipment and vehicles.

Current assets are likely to be used in the business within the year and include bank balances, stock and trade debtors.

Conversely, there are long-term and current creditors in the balance sheet. These are items the company owes to others. Long-term creditors are usually bank loans or other types of financing, and short-term creditors are typically trade suppliers and HMRC (VAT, PAYE etc).

As stated above, Assets – Liabilities = Capital. Capital is the owners' funds, and typically consist of profit and loss and other reserves and share capital (for limited companies).

Budgeting and Forecasting

In addition to the statutory accounts above, most successful businesses prepare budgets and cash flow forecasts.

Budgets are typically prepared by looking at income and expenditure for the previous year and adding (or subtracting) a percentage mark-up to next year's forecast accounts. These are then compared to the actual expenditure throughout the year and adjustments made as required.

A very simple budget is shown below:

Budget Variance   For the 12 months ended 31 August 2021

	Actual	Budget	Var GBP	Var %	YTD Actual	YTD Budget	Var GBP	Var %
Income								
Other Revenue	-	-	-	0.0%	3,500	-	3,500	0.0%
Sales	37,637	23,500	14,137	60.2%	38,470	23,500	14,970	63.7%
Total Income	**37,637**	**23,500**	**14,137**	**60.2%**	**41,970**	**23,500**	**18,470**	**78.6%**
Less Cost of Sales								
Purchases	1,950	1,500	450	30.0%	1,950	1,500	450	30.0%
Total Cost of Sales	**1,950**	**1,500**	**450**	**30.0%**	**1,950**	**1,500**	**450**	**30.0%**
Gross Profit	**35,687**	**22,000**	**13,687**	**62.0%**	**40,020**	**22,000**	**18,020**	**82.0%**
Less Operating Expenses								
Advertising & Marketing	8,711	11,000	(2,289)	-20.8%	8,711	11,000	(2,289)	-20.8%
Audit & Accountancy fees	141	150	(9)	-6.1%	141	150	(9)	-6.1%
Bank Fees	30	90	(60)	-66.7%	30	90	(60)	-66.7%
Cleaning	99	300	(201)	-66.9%	99	300	(201)	-66.9%
Consulting	-	-	-	0.0%	3,600	-	3,600	0.0%
Entertainment - 0%	-	150	(150)	-100.0%	-	150	(150)	-100.0%
Entertainment-100% business	45	-	45	0.0%	45	-	45	0.0%
General Expenses	418	360	58	16.2%	8,418	360	8,058	2238.4%
Light, Power, Heating	1,098	990	108	10.9%	1,282	990	292	29.5%
Motor Vehicle Expenses	649	390	259	66.5%	649	390	259	66.5%
Postage, Freight & Courier	94	150	(56)	-37.2%	94	150	(56)	-37.2%
Printing & Stationery	84	60	24	39.5%	596	60	536	892.8%
Rent	3,938	3,090	848	27.4%	3,938	3,090	848	27.4%
Repairs & Maintenance	886	300	586	195.4%	886	300	586	195.4%
Subscriptions	1,235	2,200	(965)	-43.9%	1,235	2,200	(965)	-43.9%
Telephone & Internet	164	135	29	21.8%	164	135	29	21.8%
Travel - National	231	450	(219)	-48.7%	231	450	(219)	-48.7%
Total Operating Expenses	**17,824**	**19,815**	**(1,991)**	**-10.0%**	**30,119**	**19,815**	**10,304**	**52.0%**
Net Profit	**17,863**	**2,185**	**15,678**	**718.0%**	**9,901**	**2,185**	**7,716**	**353.0%**

Cash flow forecasts similarly look at the cash expenditure for a given period, usually a year (but can be a month or quarter), broken down into monthly income and expenditure categories and predicted monthly income and expenditure inserted for each month.

This is mostly based on a mixture of past income and outgoings and knowledge of any changes in the coming period.

As the year goes on, the actual amounts are inserted to ensure the amounts are kept as accurate and relevant as possible.

An example is shown below:

Cash Flow Forecast

Starting cash on hand	10,000.00		Starting date	Sep-21		Cash minimum balance alert	2,000.00							
Cash on hand (beginning of month)	10,000.00	9,050.00	9,350.00		2,190.00	13,390.00	13,790.00	15,290.00	18,410.00	14,360.00	16,560.00	18,760.00		

Cash Receipts

														Flow
Cash sales	2,500.00	3,000.00	3,600.00	3,000.00	14,000.00	6,000.00	3,000.00	2,800.00	3,500.00	4,000.00	3,800.00	4,200.00		53,400.00
Returns and allowances			200.00											200.00
Collections on accounts receivable														0.00
Interest, other income														0.00
Loan proceeds														0.00
Owner contributions														0.00
Other receipts														0.00
Total Cash Receipts	2,500.00	3,000.00	3,400.00	3,000.00	14,000.00	6,000.00	3,000.00	2,800.00	3,500.00	4,000.00	3,800.00	4,200.00		53,600.00
Total Cash Available	12,500.00	11,050.00	12,750.00	3,890.00	16,190.00	19,390.00	16,790.00	18,090.00	19,910.00	18,360.00	20,360.00	22,960.00		

Cash Paid Out

Advertising	3,000.00													3,000.00
Commissions and fees	200.00	300.00	380.00	300.00	1,400.00	400.00	300.00	280.00	350.00	400.00	380.00	420.00		5,140.00
Subcontractors		200.00		200.00		200.00		200.00		200.00		200.00		1,200.00
Staff benefits														0.00
Insurance (other than health)			4,000.00			4,000.00			4,000.00			4,000.00		16,000.00
Interest expense														0.00
Materials and supplies (in COGS)	1,200.00	1,200.00	7,500.00	1,200.00	1,200.00	1,200.00	1,200.00	1,200.00	1,200.00	1,200.00	1,200.00	1,200.00		20,700.00
Meals and entertainment														0.00
Mortgage interest														0.00
Office expenses														0.00
Print, post and stationery														0.00
Pension contributions														0.00
Rent														0.00
Rates														0.00
Vehicle or equipment leasing														0.00
Repairs and maintenance														0.00
Supplies (not in COGS)														0.00
Taxes														0.00
Travel														0.00
Utilities														0.00
Wages														0.00
Other expenses														0.00
Other expenses														0.00
Other expenses														0.00
Miscellaneous														0.00
Subtotal	4,400.00	1,700.00	11,880.00	1,700.00	2,600.00	5,800.00	1,500.00	1,960.00	5,550.00	1,800.00	1,580.00	5,820.00		46,040.00
Loan repayments														0.00
Capital purchases														0.00
Other startup costs														0.00
To reserves														0.00
Owners' withdrawals														0.00
Total Cash Paid Out	4,450.00	1,700.00	11,880.00	1,700.00	2,800.00	5,800.00	1,500.00	1,680.00	5,550.00	1,800.00	1,680.00	5,820.00		46,040.00
Cash on hand (end of month)	8,050.00	9,350.00	870.00	2,190.00	13,390.00	13,790.00	15,290.00	16,410.00	14,360.00	16,560.00	18,760.00	17,090.00		

Management Accounting

The main difference between financial and management accounting is that where financial accounting aims to provide information to users outside the organisation, management accounting is intended to help managers inside the business make better and more informed decisions.

Therefore, management accounting is more flexible and not subject to the rules and regulations that financial accounts must conform to. The main objective is to tell you, the manager, what you need to know to keep your business successful and profitable.

A typical example of the difference in reporting is with sales: in financial accounting, this tends to be all shown under the heading Turnover, whereas in management accounting, it is generally more helpful to break down the sales into categories. For instance, landscape gardeners may find that breaking down sales into consultation fees, product sales, and landscape contracting fees will provide more useful information. It may well be that product sales could be broken down further to find out what it is worth concentrating their efforts on.

KPIs

The most useful reason for management accounting is that it allows the use of KPIs (Key Performance Indicators). These are quantifiable measures of key areas of your business. They should follow the SMART acronym that was discussed earlier: Specific, Measurable, Achievable, Realistic and Time-related.

Which KPIs are useful for a business will vary but usually include:

- *Gross Profit Margin (%): (Turnover – Direct Costs)/Turnover x 100*

- *Net Profit Margin (%): (Turnover – All expenses)/Turnover x 100*
- *Sales Growth %: (Turnover this period – Turnover last period)/Turnover last period*

Another area where KPIs are very useful is not directly related to financial information but rather to the business itself. Such useful measures would include staff attendance, machine downtime, and leads and orders gained from an advertising campaign.

KPIs are crucial in supporting your business strategy and goals as they provide a straightforward way to see if the business is achieving what you have planned.

Regardless of what you decide are the relevant KPIs for your business, you can see that by breaking down your income and expenditure into lots of detail, you will be able to get far more useful information by using KPIs.

Management accounting and KPIs are another huge subject that could easily fill this book in their own right, and there are many excellent books out there that go into far more detail. I strongly urge you to read some of them as it will significantly assist you in keeping your business on track and making the right decisions moving forward.

| 11 |

MARKETING AND BRANDING

Advertising, marketing, and branding is another large subject that I can only hope to scratch the surface of here, but which is critical to the success of your business, and which I again urge you to do further reading about.

It is far too easy to waste a lot of money on advertising without getting a decent return on your investment. As discussed in the previous chapter, KPIs are an excellent way to keep track of your return on investment for each advertising and marketing campaign. Still, there are several things you can do to avoid spending money randomly and learning by trial and error where to focus your attention.

Branding

Starting with branding, this is an area where you can spend as much or as little as you feel is appropriate, but whether or you decide to invest money by employing an agency for this or creating your own brand, the key is consistency. You need to be recognisable by having consistent branding that people will associate you with. Suppose your letterheads are different from your invoices and your website uses different colour schemes, fonts etc from the rest. In that case, it quickly becomes confusing for customers and potential customers to know who they are dealing with.

There are many useful resources on the internet these days, such as Canva, that can help you find branding that resonates with you and your business without having to go to the considerable expense of employing an agency.

Advertising and Marketing

Once you have your branding sorted, you will be looking at the best way to advertise and promote your business. As you have probably already discovered, there are many options when it comes to advertising, from TV and radio, through magazines, newspapers, to Facebook and right down to the card in the window at your local newsagent.

Before you dive straight in and randomly throw money at it, my advice is to utilise the information you already gathered when putting together your business plan, as this will help decide on a successful advertising strategy.

Take a close look at your target customers, and then spend some time considering where they are likely to look for your services or product and where you are likely to catch their attention. If you are selling to consumers, your advertising target will be quite different from one aimed at business-to-business selling.

Planning your advertising and marketing strategy is very useful and also helps you budget for it. Depending on your business, anything from 3 to

12 months in advance is usually key to success, especially if your product is seasonal; when planning the campaign well in advance will be likely to pay dividends. For example, if you are likely to make more sales for Christmas, you should be looking at getting your name out there around October, and likewise, if your product or service is more geared to the summer, then springtime is the time to start advertising when people are beginning to think about summer.

It is also important not to forget about the many free or low-cost advertising opportunities. A website is the most important of these, as most of us go straight to the internet to check out prospective suppliers. A decent website does not need to cost you the earth in design fees. A simple site with just a few pages can be extremely effective as long as it tells the user what they need to know about you, your products and services and how to contact you. Of course, it must work, i.e. the contact form must work, the links must work, and the pages must load fast and look good on many devices, not just on a PC. Remember that many people will use their phone to browse, so it should be easy to navigate, even on a small device.

Making sure the metadata and keywords are relevant is very important to ensure you are found by search engines and is something you can do yourself, or you can pay for specialist SEO companies to push your website.

Other free advertising includes getting listed on Google My Business and creating a Facebook page and Instagram account. Getting people to review your business, either on Google, Trustpilot or your website, is also a very effective way to reassure potential customers that you are reputable and reliable.

A blog is another good way of keeping your listing high up on the search engines without incurring costs. The key to this and Facebook and Instagram pages is to make sure you keep updating them. A Facebook page whose most recent content is 3 years old will only make a potential customer wonder if you are still in business!

| 12 |

THE RIGHT MINDSET

I touched on this subject at the beginning of this book, and I will finish by revisiting it, as I firmly believe that having the right mindset will determine whether you will succeed in your business venture.

"Whether you think you can,

or you think you can't – you're right"

Henry Ford

This famous quote sums up perfectly how your mindset can make all the difference to whether you are likely to make a success of your business and of your life.

There is a clear difference between rushing into a venture headfirst and without regard to its viability, based purely on self-belief, and being determined to succeed in something that you know can be profitable and fulfilling. There is a fine line between the two, and the danger is that you can easily fall into the trap of writing off a potentially great venture through lacking in the belief that you can make a success of it.

If you have sat down and looked at the pros and cons and found that the cons are your limiting factor, then this is where having the right mindset becomes critical. You may not have the required funds to get the venture off the ground, but are there ways of getting investors involved? You may not have the full skill set required, so is there someone you know with the skills you lack that would be willing to join you in your venture? The current market is dominated by big players that you cannot possibly compete with, so is there a niche market you can cater for and grab that all-important first slice of the cake? Where there is a will, there is usually a way!

If you have read this far, I assume that you have already done the work and decided that your business venture can be successful. From now on, it is important you keep a positive mindset and focus on the business. There is no longer room for negative self-talk and doubts about your ability to make a go of your venture.

But how do you develop a positive mindset and always stay focused? Nobody is born with this skill, although some people find it easier than others, and have a naturally "half-full cup" mentality. That does not mean you cannot change and become better at it, and many people find affirmations, mindfulness, and meditation a great help on their journey towards a positive mindset.

There are many good books available on positive thinking, but Sue Stone's wonderful book, "*The Power Within You Now*", explains in detail many ways you can use to become more positive in your life and the science behind why these methods work. If you feel you could benefit from changing your mindset I strongly recommend reading this.

CONCLUSION

Now that you have finished reading this book, you will have:

- *decided whether to operate as a sole trader or a limited company*
- *worked out how you are going to fund your business*
- *learnt a little about the taxes that you may have to pay*
- *prepared a business plan*
- *identified your target customers*
- *researched your competitors*
- *learnt about employing staff and paying yourself*
- *learnt the basics of book-keeping and accounting*
- *considered branding, advertising, and marketing*
- *got business insurance*
- *looked at your health and safety*
- *decided if your business venture will come under IR35 or CIS*
- *worked on cultivating the right mindset to succeed*

I wish you every success in your chosen venture!